CAMPING ABC BOOK

Nicole Kunkel

Always be curious.

A is for awning – it keeps you dry when it's raining or shade from the sun!

B

is for bonfire to cook up yummy hotdogs!

C

is for campground – a friendly place to stay.

D is for drinks – water, juice, and milk!

E is for equipment – you never know what you will need!

𝓕 is for friends and family to keep you company.

G is for games to have some entertainment.

H is for hiking to keep your body moving!

I is for yucky insects! Ewwwwww.

J is for jacket to keep you nice and dry.

K is for kayak to get out on the water.

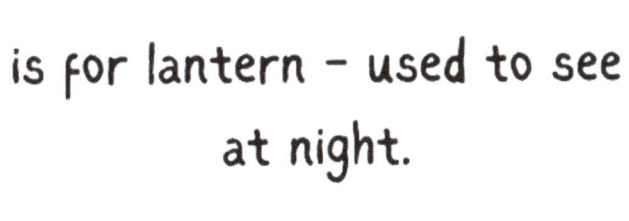 is for lantern – used to see at night.

 is for map for when you lose your way!

is for nature – get yourself outside!

O is for outhouse – hold your nose, it stinks!

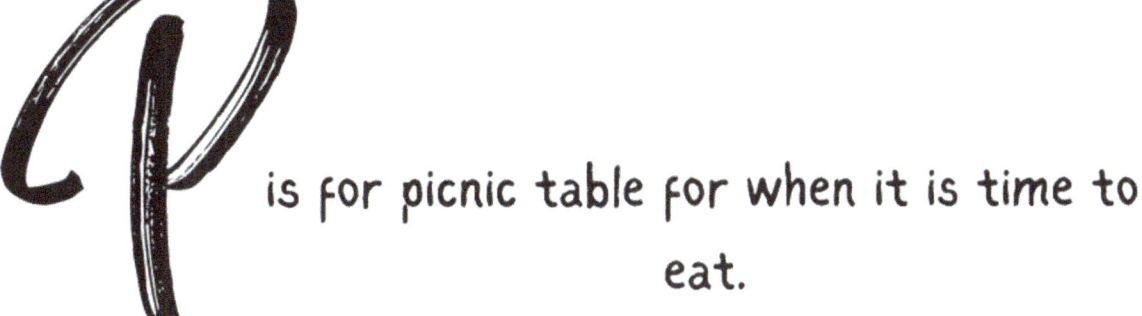

P is for picnic table for when it is time to eat.

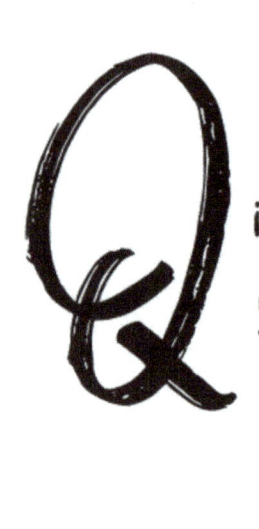

Q is for quiet - shhhh. do you hear that? Listen.

Shhh!

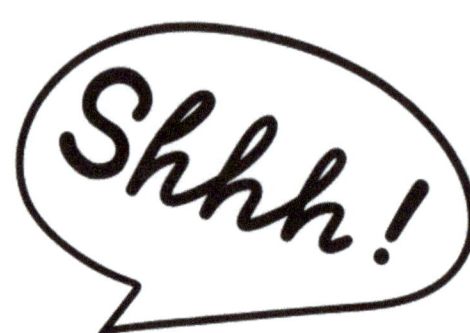

R is for RV - what a cozy place to stay.

Beep! Beep!

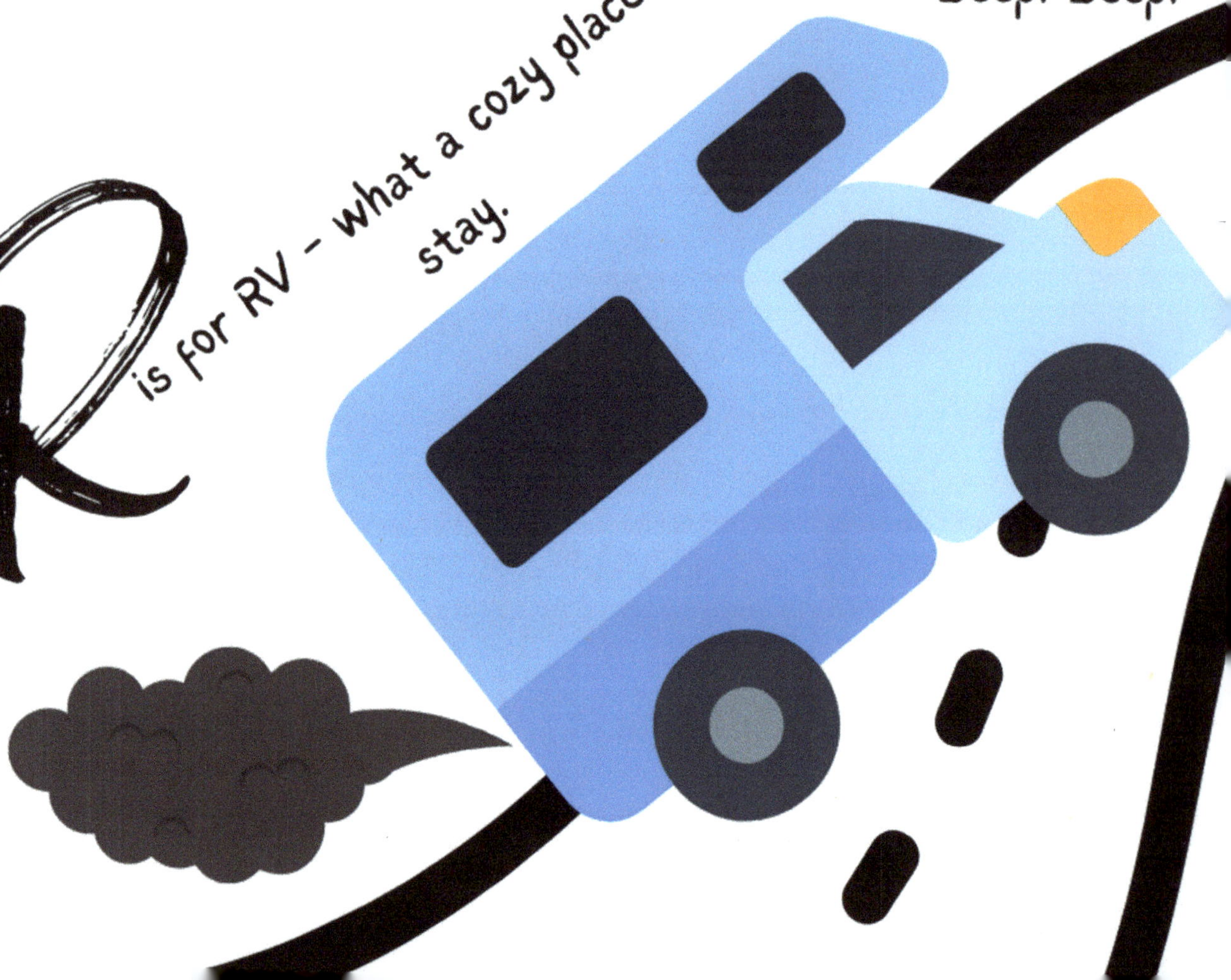

S is for s'mores. I am always looking for a tasty treat.

T is for trail – where should we go today?

U is for umbrella in case of yucky weather.

V is for vacation – even if it is only seasonal!

W is for wood to start an awesome fire.

X is for eXtinguisher for when the fire gets too wild!

 is for yurt – another style of camping.

Z is for zzz. It is time to go to bed. Let us dream about adventures that we have lying up ahead!

Question Prompts

1. Have you ever been camping?
2. What do you think the most important thing about camping is?
3. Was anything missed in this book of what we might need on a camping trip?
4. What would you bring with you on a camping trip?
5. Would you prefer a tent or a camper?
6. Who would you want with you on your camping trip?
7. When is the best time to go camping?
8. Where would you want to go camping? A campground or wilderness?
9. Why is getting outside so fun?
10. On a scale of 1-10, 10 being so excited, who would be excited to go on a camping trip?